HOUGHTON MIFFLIN

# Reading

# Comprehensive Screening
# Assessment

## Grade 2

HOUGHTON MIFFLIN

ISBN: 0-547-15305-8
ISBN: 978-0-547-15305-6
5 6 7 8 9 10 11 12 0928 17 16 15 14 13 12 11
4500295561

# Table of Contents

**Introduction** i
Administering the Comprehensive Screening Assessment iii
Scoring the Comprehensive Screening Assessment v
Assessing Students' Needs and Modifying Instruction Based on
      Comprehension and Vocabulary Scores vi
Comprehensive Screening Assessment Record Sheet vii
Notes about Additional Assessments viii
Conclusions about Student Placement viii

**Practice Test** 1
**Comprehensive Screening Assessment**
      Language Arts 3
      Phonics/Spelling 7
      Writing 10
      Comprehension/Vocabulary: Fox 12
      Comprehension/Vocabulary: Wise Owl 18
      Comprehension/Vocabulary: Count Sheep 24

Short-Response Scoring Rubrics 32

Writing Prompt Write-On-lines 34

Writing Traits Scoring Rubric 37

Qualitative Spelling Inventory 38

Qualitative Spelling Inventory Checklist 39

Transfer to Writing 41

# Introduction

## Purpose

The *Comprehensive Screening Assessment* is an initial diagnostic assessment tool designed to be administered to groups of students at the beginning of the year. It, along with informal assessment information collected during the first few weeks of school, will help you determine students' reading abilities and estimate the amount of support students are likely to need during reading instruction. In addition, student performance on this assessment will help you identify students who may need more in-depth diagnostic assessment (i.e., Houghton Mifflin's *Emerging Literacy Survey* or *Diagnostic Assessment*).

The *Comprehensive Screening Assessment* includes items that test students' comprehension, vocabulary, language arts, phonics/decoding, and writing skills. In addition, there is an optional group spelling test.

## Description

The *Comprehensive Screening Assessment* consists of a test booklet for each grade 2–6, which helps assess several key components of students' literacy abilities:

- **Language Arts** This section features 10 free-standing, multiple-choice items aligned to the grammar skills taught in the previous grade level.

- **Phonics/Decoding** This section consists of 10 free-standing, multiple-choice items that assess phonics/decoding skills taught in the previous grade level. A more in-depth phonics assessment is available as part of the *Diagnostic Assessment* for teachers who wish to get more detailed information.

- **Writing** This section features a choice of two writing prompts, one narrative and one informative, aligned to writing instruction taught at the previous grade level of *Houghton Mifflin Reading*.

- **Comprehension and Vocabulary**

     This section features three passages at the reading level of the previous grade. For example, the passages in the Grade 5 *Comprehensive Skills Assessment* are estimated to be at the 4th grade difficulty level. If students can read and understand the material from the previous grade level independently, they should be able to benefit from instruction included at the 5th grade level without a great deal of supplemental support. Each Comprehension and Vocabulary section includes a balanced mix of fiction and nonfiction.

     There are a mix of multiple-choice and short-response comprehension items after each passage that test students' understanding of what they read. These items cover both literal and inferential comprehension skills taught at the previous grade level. Additionally, there are multiple-choice vocabulary items associated with each passage as well as some free-standing, multiple-choice vocabulary items. For children who are unable to read the passages, see the individually administered *Diagnostic Assessment*.

Name _____ Date _____

# Introduction (continued)

## • Spelling

The Qualitative Spelling Inventory on page 38 enables teachers to see what students are learning by the words they spell correctly and incorrectly. Teachers can also use Feature Guide for Writing on page 41.

Words are presented in increasing difficulty. As the spelling assessment proceeds, it is evident what features students are learning by the quality of their spelling and the number of words and features they spell correctly.

# Administering the Comprehensive Screening Assessment

## Overview

The *Comprehensive Screening Assessment* should be administered by section. The sections can be administered consecutively or in more than one class period.

- If you administer the Comprehension section over more than one class period, be sure to review the Practice Test with students again.

- The writing and/or the spelling sections should be administered on a different day than the comprehension, vocabulary, phonics, and language arts sections.

## Comprehension, Vocabulary, Phonics, and Language Arts Sections

Introduce these sections by explaining that it will help *you* learn how to help *them* become expert readers. Ask them to do their best work. Explain that some parts may be difficult, but that you cannot help them with the passages or items. Assure them that they will not receive a grade, and remind them that the purpose of the assessment is to help *you* get to know *their* reading abilities.

Begin by reviewing the Practice Test with the students.

- Tell students to follow along while you read the passage aloud. Then proceed through the sample questions one by one. Blank lines follow the first question where students are to write their answers. Tell students that they should give complete answers to these types of questions using information from the stories they will read. Explain that you will be most interested in what they say and that spelling and handwriting will not count against them. Read the question aloud and have students discuss what they might write in response. Then point out that this item asks them to draw conclusions, but that other short-response items might ask students to remember a story detail, make a comparison, or explain the author's purpose.

- Questions 2 and 3 are multiple-choice questions that have one correct answer. Tell the students that they should read all the choices before they select the best one based on the story. Read each question and all the choices aloud. Then have students discuss the options and choose the best answer.

- Point out to students that sometimes an answer can be found in the story, but sometimes they need to think about what they have read and figure out an answer that is not stated in the story. Tell students that they can look back at the story at any time to get help with their answers.

Name _____  Date _____

# Administering the Comprehensive Screening Assessment (continued)

After students have completed the Practice Test, tell them that they will answer some questions about language and words. Then tell students to complete the writing task next, until they see the word STOP. Together, locate the first writing assessment and the word STOP. Then they should read the first story to themselves and answer the questions that follow it. Direct them in the same way with the second and third passages.

These tests are not timed. Allow students to finish at their own rates. If, however, some students are taking much longer than expected, you might stop them. This is one indication that these students might need more in-depth diagnostic testing.

## Writing Assessment

Before you administer the writing assessment, explain that students have a choice between Task 1 and Task 2. Remind students to plan and revise their writing before beginning their final draft on a separate sheet of paper. You might also want to distribute lined paper for these distinct steps.

## Spelling Inventory

The inventory can be given at the beginning and end of the year and one or two times in between to monitor progress. With the words in ascending difficulty, consider stopping the assessment when students make enough errors to determine a phase of spelling.

# Scoring the Comprehensive Screening Assessment

## Scoring Multiple-Choice Items

Each multiple-choice item has only one correct response and is worth 1 point.

## Scoring Short-Response Items

When you score short-response items, focus on the content and do not be distracted by mechanics, spelling, or handwriting. Acceptable responses will sometimes vary from those given in the annotations in the manual. The Scoring Rubric for Short-Response Items lists the criteria for two-point, one-point, and zero-point responses.

## Scoring Writing Prompts

Use the four-point Scoring Rubric for Writing on page 37 to score students' responses in the writing section.

## Scoring Spelling

A score of between 40% and 90% indicates that students are ready for grade level instruction.

# Assessing Students' Needs and Modifying Instruction Based on Comprehension and Vocabulary Scores

Students whose scores are between 14 and 21 should generally do well with on-level readers. Those students whose scores are higher or lower may benefit from modified instruction or additional diagnostic assessments.

- If a student scores above 21 on the comprehension and vocabulary section, consider assigning above-level readers.

- If a student scores between 14 and 21, but the results are inconsistent across narrative and expository passages or multiple-choice and short-response items, assign appropriate readers to account for the inconsistencies. For example, if a student scores high on the narrative passage items and low on the informative passage items, consider on-level or above-level readers when focusing on narrative selections and below-level readers for informative selections.

- If a student scores below 14, administer additional diagnostic testing (i.e., *Emerging Literacy Survey* or *Diagnostic Assessment*).

Teachers should monitor student progress during instruction to identify students who are struggling or who are not being challenged, and then make needed adjustments to instruction. The assessments, both formal and informal, that accompany the program are intended to help you monitor student progress and adjust your instruction during the school year.

Name _____     Date _____

## COMPREHENSIVE SCREENING ASSESSMENT RECORD SHEET

| TESTED SKILLS | ITEM NUMBERS | SCORE |
|---|---|---|
| **Language Arts** | | Total: ___ /10 |
| Singular and Plural Nouns | 1, 2, 3, 4 | ___ /4 |
| Adjectives | 5, 9 | ___ /2 |
| Kinds of Sentences | 6, 7 | ___ /2 |
| Contractions | 8, 10 | ___ /2 |
| **Phonics/Decoding** | | Total: ___ /10 |
| Short Vowels | 11, 12 | ___ /2 |
| Long Vowels | 13, 14 | ___ /2 |
| r-controlled Vowels | 15, 16 | ___ /2 |
| Digraphs | 19, 20 | ___ /2 |
| Inflectional endings | 17, 18 | ___ /2 |
| **Writing** | | Total: ___ /20 |
| Word Choice | | ___ /4 |
| Conventions | | ___ /4 |
| Spelling | | ___ /4 |
| Focus | | ___ /4 |
| Organization | | ___ /4 |
| **Comprehension** | | Total: ___ /22 |
| Drawing Conclusions | 25, 29, 44 | ___ /4 |
| Sequence of Events | 34, 40, 41 | ___ /3 |
| Cause and Effect | 39 | ___ /1 |
| Author's Purpose | 27 | ___ /1 |
| Compare and Contrast | 23, 26, 30 | ___ /4 |
| Story Structure | 33, 35, 42 | ___ /3 |
| Main Idea and Details | 22, 32, 36, 37 | ___ /6 |

Name _____ Date _____

| Vocabulary | | Total: ___ /4 |
|---|---|---|
| Context Clues | 28, 31, 38 | ___ /2 |
| Multiple-meaning Words | 24, 43 | ___ /2 |
| **Spelling Inventory** | | Total: ___ % |

# Notes About Additional Assessments

_____

_____

_____

_____

# Conclusions About Student Placement

_____

_____

_____

_____

# Practice Test

**Your teacher will tell you how to do these pages.**

### Time for a Bath

Jim and Sue wanted to give their dog a bath. They filled the tub with warm soapy water and called Sam. He did not come.

The children looked in the back yard and in the front yard. Where could Sam be? Then they looked in Jim's room.

"Look," said Sue, "I see a long fluffy tail under the bed. I know where Sam is hiding."

**1.** Why do you think Sam is hiding?

_____

- - - - - - - - - - - - - - - - - - - - - -

He doesn't want a bath.

_____

_____

- - - - - - - - - - - - - - - - - - - - - -

_____

_____

- - - - - - - - - - - - - - - - - - - - - -

_____

**2.** Where do the children find Sam?

Ⓐ in the tub

Ⓑ in the yard

Ⓒ in Jim's room

**3.** How do Jim and Sue try to find Sam?

Ⓐ They ask Mom where he is.

Ⓑ They look all over for him.

Ⓒ They fill the tub with water.

Read directions to children

**Practice Test**

# Language Arts

**Read each item.  Fill in the circle next to the correct answer.**

**1.** Read part of a sentence.

**The little girl had two red _____.**

Choose the correct form of the word to complete the sentence.

Ⓐ  balloon

Ⓑ  balloons

Ⓒ  ballooning

**2.** Read part of a sentence.

**There are many good _____ in the library.**

Choose the correct form of the word to complete the sentence.

Ⓐ  booking

Ⓑ  books

Ⓒ  book

**3.** Read part of a sentence.

**Marie and her sister like to play _____.**

Choose the correct form of the word to complete the sentence.

Ⓐ  game

Ⓑ  games

Ⓒ  gamey

Name _____ Date _____

**4.** Read part of a sentence.

**James only has one _____.**

Choose the correct form of the word to complete

the sentence.

Ⓐ brother

Ⓑ brothers

Ⓒ brotherly

**5.** Read part of a sentence.

**Last week I saw the _____ movie ever.**

Choose the correct form of the word to complete

the sentence

Ⓐ greater

Ⓑ greatest

Ⓒ greatly

**6.** Which of these sentences is a **question**?

Ⓐ All of my friends have pets.

Ⓑ Are you going to the park?

Ⓒ My brother loves pizza!

**GO ON** ➡

**7.** Which of these sentences is a **question**?

- (A) My teacher reads to us every day.
- (B) Please sit in your chair!
- (C) How many pencils are in the box?

**8.** Read the sentence.

**The man could not see over the crowd.**

What is the correct way to write the contraction for **could not**?

- (A) could'nt
- (B) couldn't
- (C) couldnt

**9.** Read part of a sentence.

**Ellen is _____ than Terrell.**

Choose the correct form of the word to complete the sentence.

- (A) tall
- (B) taller
- (C) tallest

**10.** Read the sentence.

**I do not know how to play chess.**

What is the correct way to write the contraction for

**do not**?

Ⓐ   dont'

Ⓑ   do'nt

Ⓒ   don't

Read directions to children.

**GO ON**

# Phonics/Spelling

**Read each item. Fill in the circle next to the correct answer.**

**11.** Which word has the same vowel sound as the letter

i in the word **little**?

(A)  line

(B)  pig

(C)  rain

**12.** Which word has the same vowel sound as the letter

i in the word **hill**?

(A)  bike

(B)  fish

(C)  save

**13.** Which word has the same vowel sound as the letter

a in the word **lake**?

(A)  bat

(B)  train

(C)  sea

**14.** Which word has the same vowel sound as the letters

ai in the word **mail**?

(A)  class

(B)  gate

(C)  leak

**15.** Which word has the same sound as the letters **ir** in the word **first**?

- Ⓐ ear
- Ⓑ herd
- Ⓒ tire

**16.** Which word has the same sound as the letters **ir** in the word **bird**?

- Ⓐ car
- Ⓑ porch
- Ⓒ turn

**17.** Read part of a sentence.

**We had fun _____ our bikes yesterday.**

Choose the correct form of the word to make the sentence correct.

- Ⓐ rideing
- Ⓑ riding
- Ⓒ ridding

GO ON

Name _____ Date _____

**18.** Read part of a sentence.

**The baby was _____ the rattle.**

Choose the correct form of the word to make the
sentence correct.

(A) shakking

(B) shakiing

(C) shaking

**19.** Read part of a sentence.

**The turtle hid in its _____ell.**

Choose the letters that make the word correct.

(A) ch

(B) sh

(C) th

**20.** Read part of a sentence.

**I made a wi_____ on a shooting star.**

Choose the letters that make the word correct.

(A) ch

(B) sh

(C) th

Read directions to children.

**Phonics/Spelling**

Grade 2: Comprehensive Screening Assessment

# Writing

**Choose <u>one</u> of the following writing tasks to complete.**

## Writing Task 1

One day you are looking out of your kitchen window. A bunny hops into your yard. He looks at you and waves. You go outside and talk to the bunny. Write a story about your day with the talking bunny. Where is the bunny from? What do you do together? What happens to the bunny at the end of the day?

OR

## Writing Task 2

What would you do if you woke up one morning and saw a huge ladder in your yard, reaching all the way into the clouds? Write a story about what would happen if you climbed that ladder. Where did it come from? What was at the top of the ladder? Who did you meet?

Read directions to children.

Name _____ Date _____

Before you begin, think and plan what you will write. Use the writing list to revise your writing. Then write your final story.

## Writing Checklist

_____ I gave my story a beginning, a middle, and an end.

_____ I told about the characters and about what happens to them.

_____ I used complete sentences in my story.

# Comprehension / Vocabulary

**Read this passage to learn about foxes.**

### Fox

A fox looks like a small, thin dog. Its face looks like a dog's face. Its teeth look like a dog's teeth. It has long legs, just like a dog.

The fox knows how to hunt. This animal can see and hear quite well. The fox has a good sense of smell, too. It hunts mice and rats, as well as birds and frogs. A fox will eat just about anything it can catch.

Read directions to children.

Fox cubs drink their mother's milk. Cubs stay in their den at first. Then they go out to learn to hunt. Cubs pounce on sticks and on each other. But they may pounce on mice, too.

This fox is a red fox. It hunts like a cat. Like a cat, the red fox can see well at night. If the fox spots a mouse, it stops and stays very still. Then it pounces, like a cat.

This fox is a gray fox. Its coat is black and white. Its
tail has a black tip. This fox is also called a tree fox. It
can climb trees, like a cat!

The fox looks like a dog in most ways. But sometimes,
it acts like a cat!

**GO ON ➡**

**Read and answer each item. You may look back at the story and the pictures to help you with your answers.**

**22.** Which animal is this story about?

Ⓐ the cat

Ⓑ the dog

Ⓒ the fox

**23.** Which of these animals is **most** like a fox?

Ⓐ

Ⓑ

Ⓒ

GO ON ➡

**24.** Read the sentence from <u>Fox</u>.

**If the fox spots a mouse, it stops and stays
very still.**

What does the word **spots** means in this sentence?

- Ⓐ marks on the floor
- Ⓑ to see something
- Ⓒ small colored dots

**25.** Why is the gray fox also called a **tree** fox?

- Ⓐ It eats leaves from trees.
- Ⓑ It climbs trees like a cat.
- Ⓒ It lives in trees.

**26.** How are foxes and dogs alike?

- Ⓐ Their teeth look alike.
- Ⓑ They eat the same food.
- Ⓒ They both make good pets.

**27.** The author wrote <u>Fox</u> to _____.

(A) give facts about foxes.

(B) tell a story about foxes.

(C) let people know how to save foxes

**28.** Read the sentence from <u>Fox</u>.

**Cubs pounce on sticks and on each other.**

What does the word **pounce** mean?

(A) jump

(B) run

(C) sleep

**29.** Do you think the fox is a good hunter? Why or why not?

_____

_____

_____

_____

(Use Short-response Scoring Rubric to score student's response.)

# Comprehension / Vocabulary

**Read how Owl helps the other animals in the forest.**

### Wise Owl

Owl's home was deep in the woods.  Animals came to see Owl.  Owl was wise, so he could help them.

One night, three animals came to see Owl.  Frog came first.

"Can you help me?" asked Frog.  "I can't seem to make friends."

"Well," said Owl.  "Let me think. Go home, Frog. Wait at your pond."

GO ON

Next, Moose came to see Owl. Moose, too, needed friends.

"Can you help me make friends?" Moose asked Owl.

Owl had a plan.

"I think I can help," said Owl. "Go to the pond, Moose. Get there at ten o'clock."

Then Fox came to see Owl.

"I need to make friends," sighed Fox. "Can you help?"

"Yes, yes!" hooted Owl. "But you must go to the pond. Get there at ten o'clock."

Moose and Fox got to the pond at ten o'clock.
Frog sat on his pad and croaked at them.  Owl waited
in a tree.

Then Owl swooped down.

"You each had a wish.  Each wish was the same.
Now YOU tell ME a good plan!"

"Let's be friends!" cried Frog, Moose, and Fox.

**Read and answer each item. You may look back at the story
and the pictures to help you with your answers.**

**30.** In <u>Wise Owl</u>, how are Frog, Moose, and Fox alike at
the beginning of the story? Write your answer.

_____

_____

_____

_____

Use Short-response Scoring Rubric to score student's response.

**31.** Read the sentence from <u>Wise Owl</u>.

**Then Owl swooped down.**

What does **swooped** mean?

(A) flew

(B) landed

(C) helped

**GO ON**

**32.** In <u>Wise Owl</u>, where does Owl tell the animals to go?

(A)   to the moon

(B)   to the tree

(C)   to the pond

**33.** When does the story <u>Wise Owl</u> take place?

(A)   at lunchtime

(B)   at night

(C)   in the morning

**34.** In <u>Wise Owl</u>, which animal came to see Owl first?

(A)   Fox

(B)   Frog

(C)   Moose

GO ON ➡

**Comprehension and Vocabulary**
**22**
**Grade 2: Comprehensive Screening Assessment**

**35.** In <u>Wise Owl</u>, where does Frog live?

   Ⓐ   in a tree

   Ⓑ   in a pond

   Ⓒ   in a city

**36.** In <u>Wise Owl</u>, how did Owl help his friends?

   Ⓐ   He told them all to go home.

   Ⓑ   He asked Moose to have a party at the pond.

   Ⓒ   He had them meet at the pond at the same
time.

# Comprehension / Vocabulary

Sometimes it is hard to get to sleep at night. Read this story to find out how Ben's mom tries to help Ben fall asleep.

**Count Sheep**

Ben is just a little cub. He is in his den now. He's in bed but he can't sleep. Ben's mom sings to him. Still, Ben does not go to sleep.

Read directions to children.

Ben's mom reads to him.  She reads and reads.

Then she peeks in Ben's bed.  Ben is not sleeping yet.

"Count sheep," Mom tells him. "Count with me, Ben.
One, two, three. . . ." Still, Ben does not go to sleep.

GO ON ➡

"Are you sleeping, Mom?" asks Ben. Ben's mom does
not say a thing. Do you think she is sleeping?

Name _____ Date _____

**Read and answer each item. You may look back at the story
and the pictures to help you with your answers.**

**37.** Fill in the web with details from <u>Count Sheep</u> that tell
how Ben's mom tries to get him to sleep.

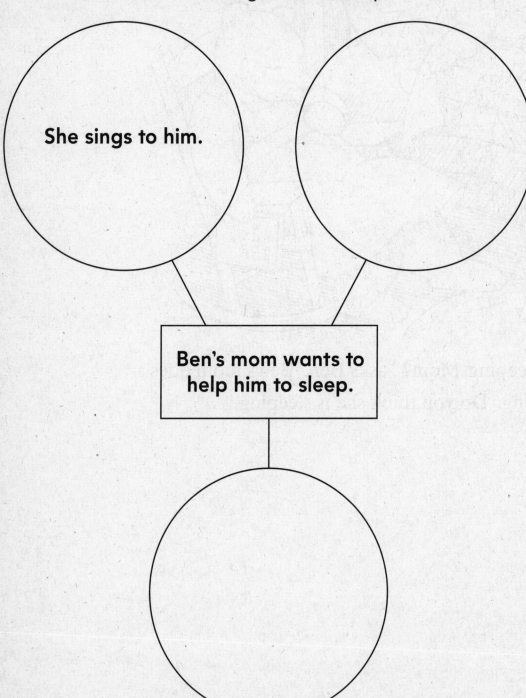

GO ON

**38.** Read the sentences from <u>Count Sheep</u>.

**Ben's mom reads to him. Then she peeks in
Ben's bed.**

What does **peeks** mean?

Ⓐ looks

Ⓑ finds

Ⓒ hides

**39.** Why does Ben's mom want him to count sheep?

Ⓐ to help him fall asleep

Ⓑ to learn how to count

Ⓒ to learn about sheep

**40.** What happened at the end of <u>Count Sheep</u>?

Ⓐ Ben fell asleep.

Ⓑ Ben went out to play.

Ⓒ Ben's mother fell asleep.

**41.** In <u>Count Sheep</u>, what was the **first** thing Ben's mother did to help him go to sleep?

  Ⓐ  sang him a song

  Ⓑ  read him a book

  Ⓒ  told him to count sheep

**42.** Where does <u>Count Sheep</u> take place?

  Ⓐ  in the forest

  Ⓑ  in Ben's room

  Ⓒ  in Mom's room

**43.** Read the sentence from <u>Count Sheep</u>.

**He is in his den now.**

What does the word **den** mean in this sentence?

  Ⓐ  a room in a house

  Ⓑ  a group of boys

  Ⓒ  a place where animals live

**GO ON**

Read directions to children.

**44.** What do you think Ben's mother will do the next time
Ben cannot fall asleep?

   Ⓐ    She will have him count sheep.

   Ⓑ    She will sing him a song.

   Ⓒ    She will try something new.

# Short-Answer Scoring Rubric for Item 29

| Score | Description |
|---|---|
| 2 | Student states and shows that a fox is a good hunter and provides one or more reasons why the fox is a good hunter. Student uses examples from the selection to support the response.<br>Examples from the story that support the explanation<br>• The fox can see and hear well.<br>• The fox has a good sense of smell.<br>• The fox can see well at night.<br>• Foxes also know how to pounce on mice. |
| 1 | Student states that the fox is a good hunter, but provides no examples to support this. |
| 0 | Student's response is totally incorrect or irrelevant. |
| B | Blank – no answer |

# Short-Answer Scoring Rubric for Item 30

| Score | Description |
|---|---|
| 2 | Student states that the animals all wanted friends and all went to Owl for help. Student uses examples from the selection to support the response.<br>Examples from the story that support the explanation<br>• All three animals want to have friends<br>• All three animals go to Owl for help |
| 1 | Student simply states that the animals are all friends but does not tell how they are alike at the beginning of the story. |
| 0 | Student's response is totally incorrect or irrelevant. |
| B | Blank – no answer |

Name _____  Date _____

# Short-Answer Scoring Rubric for Item 37

| Score | Description |
|---|---|
| 2 | Student provides two details from <u>Count Sheep</u> that tells how Ben's mom tries to get him to sleep.<br>Examples:<br>• Ben's mom reads to him.<br>• Ben's mom counts to him. |
| 1 | Student provides one detail from <u>Count Sheep</u> that tells how Ben's mom tries to get him to sleep. |
| 0 | Student's response is totally incorrect or irrelevant. |
| B | Blank – no answer |

**Short-answer Document**
Copyright © Houghton Mifflin Company. All rights reserved.

**33**

**Grade 2: Comprehensive Screening Assessment**

# Writing Prompt

# Writing Prompt (continued)

_____

- - - - - - - - - - - - - - - - - - - - - - -

_____

- - - - - - - - - - - - - - - - - - - - - - -

_____

- - - - - - - - - - - - - - - - - - - - - - -

_____

- - - - - - - - - - - - - - - - - - - - - - -

_____

- - - - - - - - - - - - - - - - - - - - - - -

_____

- - - - - - - - - - - - - - - - - - - - - - -

_____

- - - - - - - - - - - - - - - - - - - - - - -

_____

- - - - - - - - - - - - - - - - - - - - - - -

_____

- - - - - - - - - - - - - - - - - - - - - - -

_____

- - - - - - - - - - - - - - - - - - - - - - -

_____

GO ON

# Writing Prompt (continued)

_____

- - - - - - - - - - - - - - - - - - - - - - - - -

_____

- - - - - - - - - - - - - - - - - - - - - - - - -

_____

- - - - - - - - - - - - - - - - - - - - - - - - -

_____

- - - - - - - - - - - - - - - - - - - - - - - - -

_____

- - - - - - - - - - - - - - - - - - - - - - - - -

_____

- - - - - - - - - - - - - - - - - - - - - - - - -

_____

- - - - - - - - - - - - - - - - - - - - - - - - -

_____

- - - - - - - - - - - - - - - - - - - - - - - - -

_____

- - - - - - - - - - - - - - - - - - - - - - - - -

_____

- - - - - - - - - - - - - - - - - - - - - - - - -

_____

- - - - - - - - - - - - - - - - - - - - - - - - -

_____

- - - - - - - - - - - - - - - - - - - - - - - - -

# Writing Traits Scoring Rubric

| | 4 Excellent | 3 Good | 2 Fair | 1 Unsatisfactory |
|---|---|---|---|---|
| **Word Choice** | Words are colorful and used accurately. | Most words are colorful and used accurately. | Some words are colorful and used accurately. | Words are vague and uninteresting. |
| **Conventions** | Correct punctuation and sentence structure are used throughout. | Correct punctuation and sentence structure are used. | Correct punctuation and sentence structure are rarely used. | Correct punctuation and sentence structure are not used. |
| **Spelling** | All words are spelled correctly. | Most words are spelled correctly. | Some words are spelled correctly. | Most words are spelled incorrectly. |
| **Focus** | There are plenty of details that tell what, who, why, when, and where. | There are sufficient details that tell what, who, why, when, and where. | There are not enough details that tell what, who, why, when, and where. | There are no facts or exact details. |
| **Organization** | Sentences are in order and tell about the main idea. | Sentences are in order. Most tell about the main idea. | The main idea is not clear. Some sentences may not be in order. | There is no main idea and sentences are out of order. |

# Qualitative Spelling Inventory

| Level I Grade 1 | Level II Grade 2 | Level III Grade 3 | Level IV Grade 4 | Level V Grade 5 | Level VI Grade 6 |
|---|---|---|---|---|---|
| 1 net | 1 class | 1 paint | 1 shown | 1 scowl | 1 pledge |
| 2 pig | 2 went | 2 find | 2 thirst | 2 beneath | 2 advantage |
| 3 job | 3 chop | 3 comb | 3 lodge | 3 pounce | 3 changeable |
| 4 bell | 4 when | 4 knife | 4 curve | 4 brighten | 4 inspire |
| 5 trap | 5 milk | 5 scratch | 5 suit | 5 disgrace | 5 conference |
| 6 chin | 6 shell | 6 crawl | 6 bounce | 6 poison | 6 relying |
| 7 with | 7 sock | 7 throat | 7 middle | 7 destroy | 7 amusement |
| 8 drum | 8 such | 8 voice | 8 clue | 8 weary | 8 conclusion |
| 9 track | 9 sleep | 9 nurse | 9 traced | 9 sailors | 9 carriage |
| 10 bump | 10 boat | 10 weigh | 10 hurry | 10 whistle | 10 advertisement |
| 11 smoke | 11 size | 11 waving | 11 noisier | 11 chatting | 11 description |
| 12 pool | 12 plain | 12 letter | 12 striped | 12 legal | 12 appearance |
| 13 slide | 13 tight | 13 useful | 13 collar | 13 human | 13 cooperate |
| 14 shade | 14 knife | 14 tripping | 14 medal | 14 abilities | 14 democratic |
| 15 brave | 15 start | 15 early | 15 skipping | 15 decided | 15 responsible |
| 16 white | 16 fought | 16 dollar | 16 palace | 16 settlement | 16 invisible |
| 17 pink | 17 story | 17 mouthful | 17 civil | 17 surround | 17 official |
| 18 father | 18 clapped | 18 starry | 18 wrinkle | 18 treasure | 18 commission |
| 19 batted | 19 saving | 19 slammed | 19 fossil | 19 service | 19 civilize |
| 20 hugging | 20 funny | 20 thousand | 20 disappear | 20 confession | 20 inherited |
| | 21 patches | 21 circle | 21 damage | 21 frequency | 21 accidental |
| | 22 pinned | 22 laughter | 22 capture | 22 commotion | 22 spacious |
| | 23 village | 23 carried | 23 parading | 23 evidence | 23 sensibility |
| | 24 pleasure | 24 happiest | 24 trouble | 24 predict | 24 composition |
| | 25 question | | 25 imagine | 25 community | 25 accomplish |
| | | | 26 favorite | 26 president | 26 opposition |
| | | | | 27 responsible | |
| | | | | 28 sensibility | |
| | | | | 29 symphonies | |
| | | | | 30 permission | |

**38**
**Grade 2: Comprehensive Screening Assessment**

Name _____ Date _____

# Qualitative Spelling Inventory Checklist

This checklist can assist you in identifying a phase of spelling development for each student and whether the student is in the early, middle, or late part of that phase.

This checklist is particularly useful to assess spelling in students' first draft writing. This checklist can also be used to interpret students' spelling on the Qualitative Spelling Inventory on page 38 of this book.

When a feature is regularly spelled correctly, check "Yes." If the feature is spelled incorrectly or is omitted, check "No." The last feature that you checked "Often" corresponds to the student's phase of development.

## Alphabetic Phase

### Early
• Are beginning and ending consonants included?    Yes ____    Often ____    No ____

• Is there a vowel in each word?    Yes ____    Often ____    No ____

### Middle
• Are consonant digraphs and blends correct? (**sh**ade/**tr**ack)    Yes ____    Often ____    No ____

### Late
• Are short vowels spelled correctly? (h**i**d, c**o**p, s**u**ch)    Yes ____    Often ____    No ____

• Are *m* and *n* included in front of other consonants? (bu**m**p, pi**n**k)    Yes ____    Often ____    No ____

## Within-Word Pattern Phase

### Early
• Are long-vowel spellings in single-syllable words "used but confused"? (*SLIED* for *slide*, *MAIK* for *make*)    Yes ____    Often ____    No ____

• Is there a vowel in each word?    Yes ____    Often ____    No ____

### Middle
• Are most long vowels in single-syllable words spelled correctly but some long-vowel spellings still "used but confused"? (*MANE* for *main*)    Yes ____    Often ____    No ____

### Late
• Are *r*- and *l*- influenced vowels in single-syllable words spelled correctly? (st**ar**t/m**il**k)    Yes ____    Often ____    No ____

GO ON

# Qualitative Spelling Inventory
# Checklist (continued)

## Syllables and Affixes Phase

### Early
- Are inflectional endings added correctly to base
  words with short-vowel patterns? (hug**ging**, pin**ned**)

Yes ____   Often ____   No ____

### Middle
- Are inflectional endings added correctly to base
  words with long-vowel patterns? (wa**ving**, stri**ped**)

Yes ____   Often ____   No ____

### Late
- Are unaccented final syllables spelled correctly?
  (cat**tle**, accu**rate**)

Yes ____   Often ____   No ____

- Are less frequent prefixes and suffixes spelled
  correctly? (**con**fession, **pro**duction, cap**ture**, coll**ar**)

Yes ____   Often ____   No ____

## Derivational Relations Phase

### Early
- Are polysyllabic words spelled correctly?
  (expansion, community)

Yes ____   Often ____   No ____

### Middle
- Are unaccented vowels in derived words spelled
  correctly? (proh**i**bition, opp**o**sition)

Yes ____   Often ____   No ____

### Late
- Are words from derived forms spelled correctly?
  (comp**e**tition, conf**i**dent)

Yes ____   Often ____   No ____

- Are absorbed prefixes spelled correctly?
  (**ir**relevant, a**cc**omplish)

Yes ____   Often ____   No ____

GO ON ➡

# Transfer to Writing

Writing is where the depth of student learning is observed. After students study the spelling words and the underlying principles, look for them to spell related words correctly in their writing. Clearly, the transfer of student learning from spelling to writing takes time and repeated experiences over several weeks. Students' spelling in their writing is the best evidence that they have learned to spell using the principles they have studied in the weekly spelling tests.

Use the Qualitative Spelling Inventory Feature Guide to determine a feature score and developmental spelling phase for each student.

## Feature Guide for Writing

- What features did the student use correctly in writing?
- Match the features students spell correctly using the Guide below.
- Consider word study instruction when students only occasionally include the features.
- Compare this scoring to the results of the Qualitative Spelling Inventory.

| Phase | ALPHABETIC | WITHIN-WORD PATTERN | SYLLABLES & AFFIXES | SYLLABLES & AFFIXES | SYLLABLES & AFFIXES | DERIVATIONAL RELATIONS |
|---|---|---|---|---|---|---|
| | Early Middle Late | Middle Late | Early | Middle | Late | Early Middle Late |
| **Features** | Beginning & ending consonant digraphs & blends | Long vowel patterns & other vowel patterns | Less frequent vowel patterns, Prefixes & suffixes, Inflectional endings, Common syllable patterns, Unaccented syllables | Complex prefixes & suffixes, Less frequent unaccented final syllables | Spelling-meaning connection in base & derived words, Greek & Latin word parts, Absorbed prefixes |